Let's Go to the Planets!

Jacqueline Mitton

OXFORD
UNIVERSITY PRESS

OXFORD
UNIVERSITY PRESS

Great Clarendon Street, Oxford OX2 6DP

Oxford University Press is a department of the University of Oxford.
It furthers the University's objective of excellence in research, scholarship,
and education by publishing worldwide in

Oxford   New York

Auckland   Cape Town   Dar es Salaam   Hong Kong   Karachi
Kuala Lumpur   Madrid   Melbourne   Mexico City   Nairobi
New Delhi   Shanghai   Taipei   Toronto

With offices in

Argentina   Austria   Brazil   Chile   Czech Republic   France   Greece
Guatemala   Hungary   Italy   Japan   Poland   Portugal   Singapore
South Korea   Switzerland   Thailand   Turkey   Ukraine   Vietnam

Oxford is a registered trade mark of Oxford University Press
in the UK and in certain other countries

British Library Cataloguing in Publication Data

Data available

ISBN 978-0-19-917950-3

9 10 8

Printed in China by Imago

Acknowledgements

The publisher would like to thank the following for permission to reproduce
photographs: **p10** Science Photo Library. All other photographs by: NASA

Cover photograph by: Classet/OUP

Illustrations by: **p5, p8, p9** Barking Dog Art

Design by John Walker

Every effort has been made to contact copyright holders of material reproduced in this book. If notified,
the publishers will be pleased to rectify any errors or omissions at the earliest opportunity

Contents

We have lift-off! 4

A solar system to explore 6

Are we on track? 8

Race to the Moon 10

One small step 12

Mercury, *Mariner* and *Messenger* 14

Through the clouds of Venus 16

Return to the Red Planet 18

Rendezvous with an asteroid 20

Galileo goes to Jupiter 22

Cassini meets Saturn 24

Huygens drops in on Titan 26

Voyaging to the edge 28

Think about it! 30

Glossary 31

Index 32

We have lift-off!

Imagine the scene. About a hundred people are sitting on a stand overlooking a vast open field. It looks almost as if a sports match is about to begin. But all eyes are on a distant tower. From so far away, the rocket looks very small even though it is 50 metres tall. The safety officer forbids spectators to go any nearer.

There's an air of excitement but some people can't hide their anxiety. They are scientists who have spent years preparing for today. Their spacecraft is in the top of the rocket, waiting to be launched. It has been tested over and over again but will it survive its long journey through space?

A rocket launches the Stardust spacecraft on a mission to a comet in 1999.

Now a voice over the loudspeaker is saying, "Ten, nine, eight, seven, six, five…" Everyone falls silent. "Four, three, two, one, lift-off! We have lift-off!" There's a flash, then a roar. Smoke billows from the base of the rocket. Slowly at first, the launch vehicle leaves the ground. Gaining speed, it soars upward. Moments later, it's a speck in the sky. Then it's gone.

2.9 metres

Outer cover (Fairing)

Spacecraft

3rd stage solid fuel rocket

2nd stage liquid fuel tanks

2nd stage engine

38 metres

1st stage liquid fuel tanks

Solid fuel booster rocket

1st stage engine

Escaping from Earth

If you throw a ball up, it falls down again because Earth's **gravity** pulls it back. To escape from Earth and keep travelling on into space, your ball would have to reach a speed of 11.2 kilometres per second, or more than 25,000 miles per hour! To get up to such a high speed, rockets have very powerful engines and they use an enormous amount of fuel.

A rocket is mostly fuel and engines. The small spacecraft sits at the top. The bottom stages of the rocket fall away after their fuel is used up.

A solar system to explore

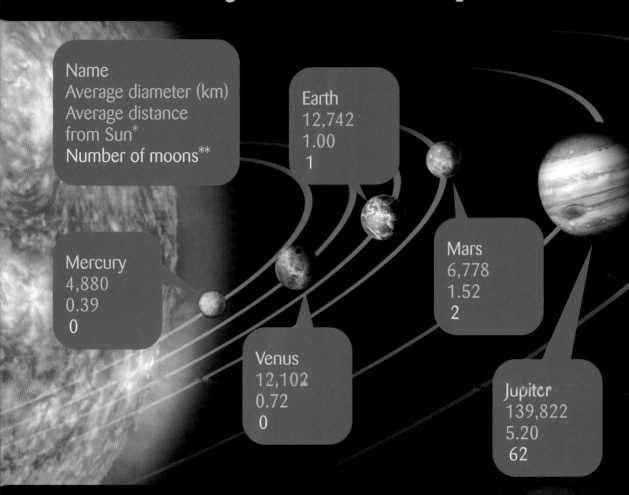

Name
Average diameter (km)
Average distance
from Sun*
Number of moons**

Earth
12,742
1.00
1

Mercury
4,880
0.39
0

Mars
6,778
1.52
2

Venus
12,102
0.72
0

Jupiter
139,822
5.20
62

Our **planet**, Earth, belongs to the solar system – a large family of worlds in **orbit** around the Sun. Besides Earth there are eight more planets. Six of them have their own families of **moons**. Then there are **asteroids** and **comets**, which are smaller than the major planets. They are all exciting places to explore. We can learn a lot by studying them through telescopes but it's much better to send spacecraft. That way we can take pictures and do experiments to find out what these worlds are really like from close up.

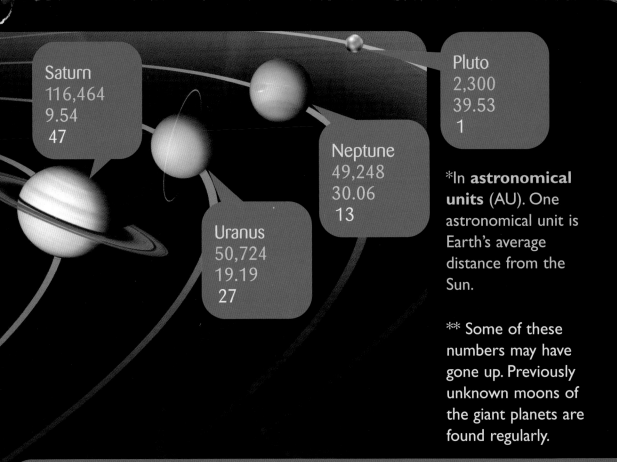

Saturn
116,464
9.54
47

Pluto
2,300
39.53
1

Neptune
49,248
30.06
13

Uranus
50,724
19.19
27

*In **astronomical units** (AU). One astronomical unit is Earth's average distance from the Sun.

** Some of these numbers may have gone up. Previously unknown moons of the giant planets are found regularly.

Where can we go?

- Earth-like planets – Mercury, Venus, and Mars: these are small and rocky, like Earth, on orbits near the Sun.

- Giant planets – Jupiter, Saturn, Uranus (say *you-ran-uss*) and Neptune: these are chiefly gas on the outside and liquid lower down. They are on orbits far apart and very distant from the Sun.

- Icy dwarfs – Pluto and the Kuiper (say *koy-per*) Belt: a swarm of thousands of little, icy asteroids beyond Neptune. Pluto is one of the biggest of them.

- Moons: there are at least 150. Earth's Moon and six others are as large as small planets.

- Asteroids: these are hundreds of thousands of miniature rocky worlds, most orbiting the Sun between Mars and Jupiter.

- Comets: these are icy dwarfs from beyond Neptune that stray close to the Sun and grow tails of gas and dust.

Are we on track?

All down to gravity

The planets stay in their orbits because the Sun's gravity keeps pulling at them. When a spacecraft sets off from Earth to travel to another planet it goes into an orbit round the Sun too. In these simple diagrams, the orbits of the planets are drawn as circles around the Sun. In actual fact, the orbits of planets and spacecraft are elliptical – shaped like squashed circles.

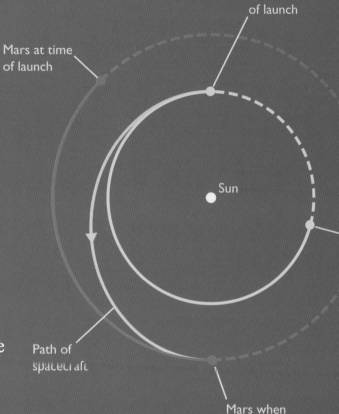

Earth at time
of launch

Mars at time
of launch

Sun

Path of
spacecraft

Mars when
spacecraft arrives

- - - - Earth's orbit
- - - - Mars' orbit

Planning the journey

A mission to another planet, such as Mars, follows a curved path through space. At lift-off, it is no use pointing towards the planet you want to visit. By the time the spacecraft gets there, the planet will have moved! Mission planners have to calculate exactly the right speed and direction the spacecraft must have in order to put it on course for its target.

Gravity gives a helping hand

Sometimes a spacecraft needs an extra spurt of speed and a change of direction. A close swing around a planet can give it just the right boost – and without using any fuel. It works because the spacecraft temporarily gets caught alongside the planet and picks up some of the planet's motion as it speeds around the Sun. Doing this is called 'gravity assist'. To help it reach Saturn, the *Cassini* (say *cass-ee-nee*) mission to Saturn swung close by Venus twice, once by Earth and once by Jupiter.

Into orbit around Saturn (Jul 2004)

Jupiter flyby (Dec 2000)

Earth when spacecraft arrives at Mars

1st Venus flyby (Apr 1998)

2nd Venus flyby (Jun 1999)

Sun

Earth flyby (Aug 1999)

Earth at time of launch (Oct 1997)

Path of Cassini spacecraft

Earth's orbit
Venus' orbit
Jupiter's orbit
Saturn's orbit

Changing course

Spacecraft carry some fuel and small jet engines so they can make course changes, or **manoeuvres** (say *man-oo-vers*). When *Cassini* reached Saturn, it fired its engines to go into an orbit around the ringed planet. In the last few years, another way to push a spacecraft along has been tested. It's called 'electric **propulsion**'.

Deep Space 1 used electric propulsion to get close to a comet in 2003. The electricity was generated by its huge **solar panels**.

Race to the Moon

The space race

Being nearest to us, the Moon was naturally the first target for spacecraft. Russia and America competed with each other. In total, they sent 40 unmanned spacecraft to the Moon between 1959 and 1969. Many of the early attempts failed.

America goes for it

In 1961, the United States decided it wanted to be the first nation to get **astronauts** to the Moon. President John F. Kennedy made a famous speech. He said:

"I believe that this nation should commit itself to achieving the goal, before this decade is out, of landing a man on the Moon and returning him safely to the Earth. No single space project in this period will be more impressive to humankind, or more important for the long-range exploration of space; and none will be so difficult or expensive to accomplish."

President Kennedy making his speech.

Some **lunar** firsts

1950

1960

1959 (October)
Luna 3 (Russia)
First pictures of the far side of the Moon

1964 (July)
Ranger 7 (USA)
First close-up pictures

Orbiters and landers

Before astronauts could go to the Moon, spacecraft had to be put into orbit to make maps, and unmanned **landers** tested what the surface was like. *Apollo 12* astronauts later went to inspect one of those landers, called *Surveyor 3*. When they arrived in November 1969, it had been on the Moon for two years and seven months.

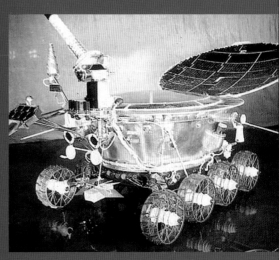

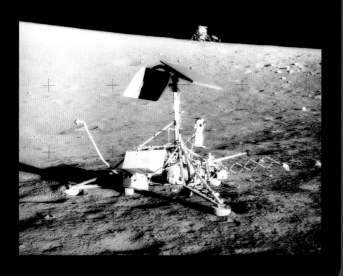

Lunokhod

The Russians concentrated on using robots to explore the Moon and fetch samples of rock. They landed mobile explorers like this one on the Moon in 1970 and 1973. These robots were called Lunokhod. They took photographs and analysed rock samples.

1966 (January)
Luna 9 (Russia)
First soft landing

1966 (March)
Luna 10 (Russia)
First artificial satellite to orbit the Moon

1969 (July)
Apollo 11 (USA)
First manned landing

1970

1980

1990

2000

1994
Clementine (USA)
First mission for 22 years returns **data** for 2 months

2004
Smart-1 (Europe)
First European mission. First to use electric propulsion

One small step

Astronauts on the Moon

The Moon is the only world beyond Earth that humans have so far explored. Neil Armstrong and Buzz Aldrin were the first there. They stepped out of their *Apollo 11* **Lunar Module** onto the Moon's surface on 20 July 1969. There were five more successful *Apollo* missions after that. The *Apollo* astronauts collected nearly 400 kilograms of lunar rocks and set up several scientific experiments. The last astronauts left the Moon in December 1972 and no one has been back since.

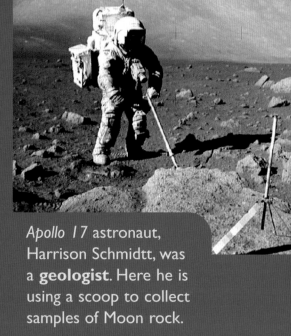

Apollo 17 astronaut, Harrison Schmidtt, was a **geologist**. Here he is using a scoop to collect samples of Moon rock.

Lunar Rover

The later *Apollo* missions took a special vehicle, nicknamed the *Lunar Rover*, so they could explore farther from their landing site.

Here, James B. Irwin, one of the *Apollo 15* astronauts, works beside the *Lunar Rover* on the Moon in July 1971.

People or machines?

Sometime in the future, human astronauts may go to the Moon again. One day, people may even venture as far as Mars or to one of the asteroids. Teams of space scientists are already working towards these goals. But other scientists disagree and argue that it is better to concentrate on exploring the solar system with unmanned spacecraft and robots.

There are good reasons both for and against sending human astronauts to explore nearby worlds such as the Moon, Mars or an asteroid.

FOR

- No machine can ever be as good at exploring as humans.
- It will help us understand much more about all planets, including Earth.
- Humans will never be satisfied until they have done it.
- It's an exciting challenge.
- The Moon is a far better place than Earth to put telescopes.

AGAINST

- It's too expensive.
- Money and resources should go towards improving things on Earth.
- You could have many robotic explorers for the same money.
- It's dangerous for the astronauts, especially going farther than the Moon.
- It doesn't help us to explore the more distant or inhospitable planets.

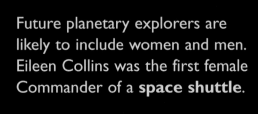

Future planetary explorers are likely to include women and men. Eileen Collins was the first female Commander of a **space shuttle**.

Mercury, *Mariner* and *Messenger*

Mariner 10

In 1973, the *Mariner 10* spacecraft set off on a journey to visit the two planets between Earth and the Sun – Mercury and Venus. *Mariner 10* was the first space mission ever to visit two planets. It was also the first spacecraft to use the gravity of one planet to help it reach another one.

The *Mariner 10* spacecraft.

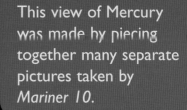

This view of Mercury was made by piecing together many separate pictures taken by *Mariner 10*.

Mercury

So far, *Mariner 10* is the only spacecraft to have returned close-up pictures of Mercury. The pictures show that Mercury is covered all over with **craters** and looks a bit like the Moon.

Venus

Venus is always covered with thick clouds made of droplets of acid. *Mariner 10* took pictures of the cloud tops but could not see what is under them. The temperature of Venus, beneath the cloud, is a sweltering 450° Celsius, and the crushing **atmosphere** presses down on Venus' surface 90 times harder than the air does on Earth. Spacecraft trying to land on Venus have to be very strong or they would be roasted and crushed at the same time!

Mariner 10's view of cloud-covered Venus.

Why is Venus so hot?

Venus' dense atmosphere is nearly all **carbon dioxide**. This gas very easily traps the heat rays coming from the Sun. What happens is called 'the greenhouse effect' because glass traps heat inside a greenhouse in the same way.

Messenger

The first mission to Mercury since *Mariner 10* is called *Messenger.* It was launched in August 2004 along a complicated path. It was designed so that first it swings round Earth. Then it skims past Venus twice before flying close by Mercury three times. After all that, in 2011 it goes into orbit around Mercury for a year.

The Messenger spacecraft.

Through the clouds of Venus

With radar eyes

If your eyes could pick up radio waves, you would be able to see through clouds. The *Magellan* spacecraft carried radar to act like 'radio eyes' for looking through Venus' clouds. *Magellan* arrived at Venus in August 1990 and went into orbit. Strip by strip, it gradually mapped all of Venus and sent the information back to Earth. In 1994, when it had finished, it was allowed to burn up.

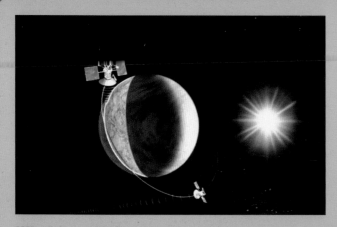

Magellan was the first mission for exploring a planet to be carried into space by a space shuttle. It was launched from the cargo bay of the shuttle *Atlantis*.

What is radar?

Radar is a made-up word. It comes from RAdio Detection And Ranging. It works by bouncing radio signals off objects. The echoes tell you the shape of the objects and how far away they are. The special radar on *Magellan* fired thousands of radio pulses a second and used a computer to turn the echoes into pictures of the hidden surface.

Volcanic Venus

Magellan revealed an amazing landscape on Venus with volcanoes, dome-like hills and weird **lava** flows. It's even possible that Venus still has active volcanoes like Earth, though we cannot be sure. There are a few craters, but not many. Venus is the only planet with the name of a goddess, so features on Venus have mostly been given female names. For example, there are craters called Alison, Chloe, Jane and Linda.

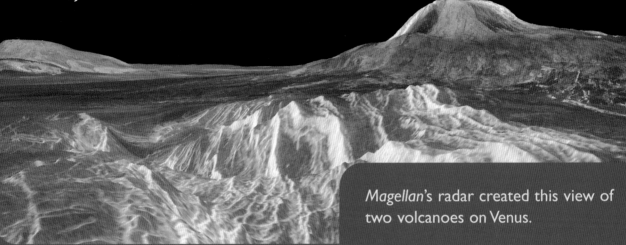

Magellan's radar created this view of two volcanoes on Venus.

A rocky landscape

Between 1961 and 1983 the Russians sent 16 spacecraft to Venus, all called *Venera (say **vee**-ner-rah)*. The first three failed but all the others sent back data. A capsule from *Venera 7* landed in December 1970. It became the first constructed object to return signals from another planet.

Venera 13 took this **panorama** of the rocky landscape around its landing site.

Return to the Red Planet

The *Hubble Space Telescope* took this view of Mars in 1999.

Mars is the planet more like Earth than any other planet and would be the first one to be visited by human explorers. Between 1960 and 2003, there were 35 attempts to send spacecraft to Mars. *Mariner 4* flew past and returned the first close-up pictures in 1965. Only half the missions to Mars have been successful. But space scientists keep trying.

Landers and orbiters

By 2005, five spacecraft had landed on Mars. Three of them have trundled across the surface on wheels. Mapping the whole planet is done from orbit. The *Viking Orbiters* gave us the first good maps in the 1970s.

Successful missions to Mars

Mariner 4   1964
Flyby
First close-ups of Mars

Mariners 6 and 7   1969
Flybys
More close-up images

Vikings 1 and 2   1975
Orbiters and Landers
First soft landers, arrived 1976

Mars Global Surveyor 1996
Orbiter
First success at Mars for 20 years; started mapping 1999

Mariner 9   1971
Orbiter
First craft to orbit another planet (1971–72)

Key
Spacecraft
Date launched
Mission type
Notes

One of the Mars *Exploration Rovers* that started to drive around in 2004.

Could there be life on Mars?

Some scientists think tiny forms of life might be able to exist underground or perhaps they were there in the past. So far no one has found any proof.

What is it like on Mars?

The landscape on Mars is like a rocky desert on Earth but with craters. There's a thin atmosphere of carbon dioxide and the sky looks pink because winds whip up the reddish dust. The north and south poles are white with ice and frost. Liquid water may have existed on Mars very long ago but there's none now – it's too cold for one thing. Mars has the largest volcano in the solar system, called *Olympus Mons*, but all Mars' volcanoes have long been extinct.

A view of Mars' surface taken in 2004 by *Spirit*, one of the *Mars Exploration Rovers*.

Mars Pathfinder 1996
Lander
First rover on Mars
(*Sojourner*); arrived 1997

Mars Exploration Rovers 2003
Landers
Rovers *Spirit* and *Opportunity*,
arrived 2004

Mars 2001 Odyssey 2001
Orbiter
Mapping composition of
Mars' surface began 2002

Mars Express 2003
Orbiter
First European mission
to Mars

Rendezvous with an asteroid

Several spacecraft have flown close to asteroids. On its way to Jupiter, *Galileo* (see pages 22–23) took close-up images of two asteroids. But so far only one spacecraft has orbited around an asteroid. That mission was called *NEAR*, short for *Near Earth Asteroid Rendezvous* (say *ron-day-voo*). It was launched in 1996 and the asteroid it visited was Eros.

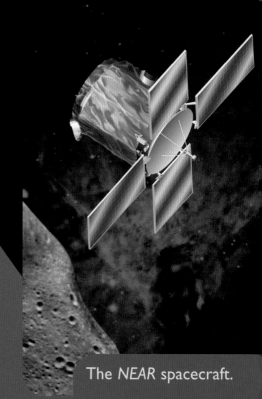

The *NEAR* spacecraft.

Near disaster

The *NEAR* spacecraft got into trouble during its journey. In December 1998, an engine burn went wrong and engineers lost all radio contact with the craft for more than a day. When they picked up signals again, *NEAR* was on the wrong path and had used up a lot of fuel. Fortunately, *NEAR* could be put back on course. It eventually got to Eros in 2000 – a year late. It stayed in orbit for a year and returned many pictures. In the end, *NEAR* was allowed to make a gentle crash landing.

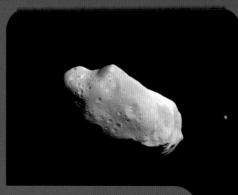

Galileo's close-up picture of asteroid Ida. Ida is 58 km long and has a tiny moon, called Dactyl.

Asteroid Eros

Eros is like a large potato-shaped rock, 33 kilometres long and 13 kilometres across. Its surface is covered with greyish dust and boulders, and it's pitted with many craters. It was probably broken off a larger object when two asteroids collided long ago.

One of *NEAR's* pictures of Eros

Near Earth Asteroids

Eros is an example of an asteroid that doesn't stay in the **asteroid belt**. It comes quite close to Earth but never gets nearer than 23 million kilometres. We know of more than 3,000 'near Earth' asteroids. Some small asteroids have come closer to Earth than the Moon. In 2004, a rock 30 metres across skimmed by Earth less than 43,000 kilometres away – that's only about one tenth the distance to the Moon.

Galileo goes to Jupiter

The *Galileo* mission to Jupiter was launched on its long journey from a space shuttle in 1989. It arrived at Jupiter in 1995 and was put into orbit. It released a **probe** that parachuted down into Jupiter's atmosphere. The main communications **antenna** on *Galileo* failed to open but the mission still returned fantastic pictures and information. In 2003, the spacecraft was deliberately crashed into Jupiter so that it wouldn't become useless junk polluting space.

How an artist imagined *Galileo* over Jupiter. What looks like a partly shut umbrella is the communication antenna that did not open properly. The blue dots represent signals coming from the probe that went down into Jupiter's atmosphere.

An artist's image of the probe released by *Galileo* going down through Jupiter's clouds.

The face of a giant

The giant planet Jupiter has dark and light belts of cloud, full of wonderful swirling patterns and oval spots of different colours. The largest and most famous feature is the Great Red Spot, which is larger than Earth and rather like a hurricane. Winds blow around it at 400 kilometres per hour (250 miles per hour).

Amazing moons

Jupiter has at least 62 moons – more than any other planet. *Galileo* specially studied its four largest ones: Io (say **eye**-oh), Europa (say *you-**rope**-ah*), Ganymede and Callisto. Io has dozens of active volcanoes and is covered with colourful lava flows. Europa is thought to have an ocean of liquid water under its icy crust. Some scientists say there could even be life in Europa's buried ocean. Ganymede is the largest moon in the solar system. Callisto is one of the most heavily cratered worlds known.

This combination of pictures taken by *Galileo* shows part of Jupiter with its Great Red Spot on the right and Jupiter's four largest moons. From top to bottom: Callisto, Ganymede, Europa, Io.

Cassini meets Saturn

Bigger than a double-decker bus, *Cassini* is the largest spacecraft ever sent to explore a planet. It should spend at least four years studying Saturn, its moons and its fantastic rings. *Cassini* was launched in 1997. To gain enough speed to reach Saturn, it used 'gravity assist' (see page 9) and made close swings past Earth and Venus. *Cassini* arrived at its destination in July 2004 and manoeuvred into orbit around Saturn. It had travelled a total of 3.5 billion kilometres, even though Saturn was only 1.5 billion kilometres away along a straight line.

This imaginary picture, made with a computer, shows *Cassini* burning its engines as it goes into orbit around Saturn.

This portrait of Saturn was made by *Cassini* in 2004. It consists of 126 separate pictures put together like tiles.

Mysterious moons

Saturn has at least 34 moons. Some of them are particularly interesting and mysterious. For instance, half of the surface of Iapetus (say *yap-ee-tuss*) is as bright as snow while the other half is as dark as night. No one knows why. It has mountains three times higher than Mount Everest. Enceladus (say *en-sell-a-duss*) is the shiniest moon in the solar system and it has a thin atmosphere of gas. This gas might be coming from icy volcanoes or **geysers**. Titan's surface is shrouded in **haze**.

Ringside spectacular

Saturn's beautiful rings are made of countless chunks of ice and bits of dust. Pictures taken close-up show many separate ringlets. The rings may be the pieces of a moon that broke up when it strayed too close to Saturn.

Cassini took this picture of Saturn's moon, Rhea, in 2005. Rhea is 1,528 km across.

Cassini controversy

Near the Sun, spacecraft can get electric power by using solar panels. But out at Saturn the sunlight is too feeble. *Cassini* is powered by three generators that use heat from radioactive material. Some people protested about the launch in case it went wrong. They thought that **radioactive plutonium** might be scattered if the spacecraft blew up. But scientists said there was no danger to Earth, and the United States government gave the go-ahead for the launch.

An ordinary picture of Titan. All you can see is its hazy atmosphere.

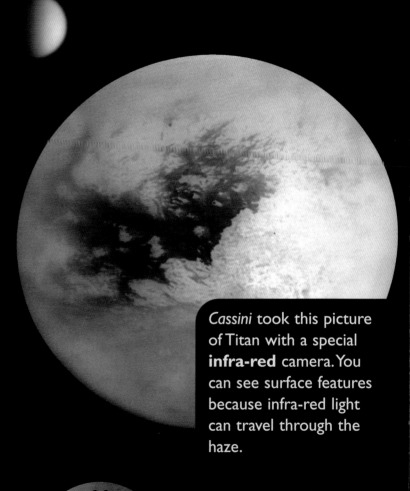

Why Is Titan so hazy?

Titan's atmosphere is mostly **nitrogen**, like Earth's, but it also has **methane** and other chemicals in it. Though the sunlight is not strong out at Saturn, it does act on the chemicals in Titan's atmosphere. Tiny particles form, and these create the haze.

Cassini took this picture of Titan with a special **infra-red** camera. You can see surface features because infra-red light can travel through the haze.

Landing on Titan

To find out more about Titan, the *Cassini* spacecraft released a special probe named *Huygens* (say **hoy**-*gens*). It landed on Titan on 14 January 2005. *Huygens* worked almost perfectly. It parachuted through Titan's atmosphere, taking pictures and data for two and a half hours as it drifted down. It then landed on soft ground and sent back another hour's worth of data. It was the most remote landing on a planet or moon ever attempted.

How an artist imagined the *Huygens* probe landing on Titan.

What Titan is like

Titan is a bit like Earth except that it has ice instead of rock and liquid methane instead of liquid water! Water is frozen as hard as rock because it's so cold (about −178° Celsius) but methane is liquid at this low temperature. *Huygens'* pictures show what look like river channels. Methane droplets probably fall from clouds, like rain. Winds on Titan are very strong, reaching hurricane force (120 kilometres per hour or 75 miles per hour).

The *Huygens* probe took this picture after it landed. You can see large pebbles made of ice.

Voyaging to the edge

The *Voyagers*

In the late 1970s and 1980s, the four giant planets – Jupiter, Saturn, Uranus and Neptune – were on the same side of the Sun. The way they lined up meant that a spacecraft could fly past them, one after another. This only happens once in over 100 years. So *Voyager 2* was sent on a tour of all four planets. It was launched in 1977 along with its twin, *Voyager 1*. *Voyager 1* only went to Jupiter and Saturn. Then it was catapulted out of the solar system by Saturn's gravity. *Voyager 2* went on to reach Uranus in 1986 and Neptune in 1989. It is the only spacecraft ever to visit those two planets.

One of the *Voyager* spacecraft.

Uranus and Neptune

Uranus and Neptune are similar sizes and look like different shades of blue. Uranus was very plain when *Voyager* went past, but Neptune had dark oval spots and little white clouds. *Voyager* also took some amazing close-up pictures of Neptune's large moon, Triton. Since *Voyager* flew past Uranus and Neptune, astronomers have followed changes on them with the *Hubble Space Telescope*.

One of the pictures *Voyager 2* took of Neptune.

Pluto – the last frontier

Pluto is the only one of the nine planets no spacecraft has visited so far. The *New Horizons* mission to Pluto is due to be launched in January 2006. It will arrive at Pluto and its moon, Charon (say *kar-ron*), in 2015.

The *New Horizons* spacecraft as it might look near Pluto.

What next?

Something new is always happening with space missions so the latest developments will soon be missing from any book. These web sites should help you to keep up to date:

http://solarsystem.nasa.gov/planets/index.cfm
http://spaceflight1.nasa.gov/mars/
http://www.esa.int/SPECIALS/Aurora/

Think about it!

Now you've read this book, here are some questions to think about. There are no right answers!

- **Should governments spend money on sending spacecraft to explore the planets? Can you think of reasons for and against it?**

- **Is it a good idea for humans to travel to the Moon and the planets?**

Who were they?

Some of the spacecraft mentioned in this book are named after these famous people.

Giovanni (say *jee-o-vann-ee*) Domenico **CASSINI** (1625–1712) was born in Italy but worked most of his life in Paris at the Observatory. He discovered four of Saturn's moons (Iapetus, Rhea, Dione (say *die-oh-nee*) and Tethys) and a gap in Saturn's rings.

GALILEO GALILEI (1564–1642) was the first person to look at the sky with a telescope. He discovered the four largest moons of Jupiter. He was born in Pisa in Italy and worked in the cities of Florence and Padua.

Christiaan **HUYGENS** (1629–1695) was a Dutch astronomer and scientist. He discovered Saturn's moon, Titan. He was also famous for inventing the pendulum clock.

Ferdinand **MAGELLAN** (1480–1521) was an explorer. He was born in Portugal but later became a Spanish citizen. He led the first expedition that managed to sail around the world but he was killed part way through the journey.

Glossary

antenna – dish or aerial for sending or picking up radio signals

asteroid – a small world orbiting the Sun

asteroid belt – the region between the orbits of Mars and Jupiter where most asteroids are found

astronaut – a human who travels into space (Russian space travellers are called cosmonauts)

astronomical unit (or AU) – a unit of measurement equal to the average distance between Earth and Sun, which is 149,597,870 kilometres. It is used for giving distances between the planets and the Sun. For example, Jupiter's average distance is 5.2 AU, which means it is just over 5 times Earth's distance from the Sun

atmosphere – a layer of gas on the outside of a planet or moon

carbon dioxide – a colourless gas found in the atmospheres of planets

comet – a small icy asteroid that releases gas and dust when it is heated by the Sun

crater – a round pit in the ground. Most craters on moons and planets have been made by high-speed rocks from space crashing down

data – information, such as facts and numbers

geologist – a scientist who studies rocks and the surfaces of planets

geyser – a natural fountain that spurts up from under the ground

gravity – a force of attraction that acts between all things

gravity assist – using the gravity of a planet to change the speed and direction of a spacecraft

haze – a mist of tiny solid particles floating in an atmosphere

Hubble Space Telescope – a telescope in orbit around Earth at a height of about 600 km

infra-red – rays similar to light but invisible to human eyes

lander – a spacecraft built to land on the surface of a moon or planet

lava – hot, molten rock that flows out from under ground then becomes solid as it cools down

lunar – to do with the Moon

Lunar Module – the part of an Apollo spacecraft that landed on the Moon

manoeuvre – an alteration to the speed and/or direction of a spacecraft

methane – the chemical we call natural gas

moon – a natural object in orbit around a planet

nitrogen – a colourless gas that makes up 80% of Earth's atmosphere

orbit – the path of a planet around the Sun, or the path of a moon or artificial satellite around a planet

orbiter – a spacecraft put into an orbit around a planet

panorama – a wide view

planet – a world in orbit around the Sun

plutonium – a radioactive material used to generate nuclear power and in nuclear bombs

probe – a small spacecraft released from a larger one to collect information about the atmosphere or surface of a planet or moon. (In the early days of spaceflight, all spacecraft sent to the Moon and planets were called probes)

propulsion – a way of pushing something forward

radioactive – naturally giving off powerful and dangerous rays

rendezvous – a meeting. Rendezvous is a French word often used in English

solar panel – a panel that converts the sunlight falling on it into electrical power

space shuttle – a re-usable American spacecraft used to carry astronauts and equipment into orbit around Earth. Space shuttles take off like rockets but land on a runway-like aircraft

Index

Apollo moon missions *11, 12*
asteroids *6, 7, 20, 21*
astronauts *11, 12, 13*
Callisto *23*
Cassini, Giovanni Domenico *30*
Cassini mission *9, 24, 25, 26, 27*
Charon *29*
comets *6, 7*
Enceladus *25*
Eros *20, 21*
Europa *23*
Galileo Galilei *30*
Galileo spacecraft *20, 22, 23*
Ganymede *23*
gravity *5, 8, 9, 24*
gravity assist *9*
Huygens, Christiaan *30*
Huygens probe *26, 27*
Iapetus *25*
Ida *20*
Io *23*
Jupiter *6, 7, 22, 23, 28*
Kennedy, President John F *10*
Kuiper Belt *7*
Lunar Rover *12*
Lunokhod *11*
Magellan, Ferdinand *30*

Magellan spacecraft *16, 17*
Mariner 10 *14*
Mars *6, 7, 18, 19*
Mars Exploration Rovers *19*
Mars missions *18, 19*
Mercury *6, 7, 14, 15*
Messenger spacecraft *15*
Moon *10, 11*
moons *6, 7*
Near Earth Asteroid Rendezvous (NEAR) spacecraft *20*
Neptune *7, 28*
New Horizons spacecraft *29*
orbits *8*
planets *6, 7*
Pluto *7, 29*
radar *16*
Rhea *25*
rocket *4, 5*
Saturn *7, 24, 25, 28*
solar system *6, 7*
Titan *25, 26, 27*
Uranus *7, 28*
Venera spacecraft *17*
Venus *6, 7, 15, 16, 17*
Voyager spacecraft *28, 29*